SPEAKING
LIKENESSES

Some Books by Maurice Lindsay

Collected Poems 1940–1990 (*Mercat Press*)
On The Face Of It: Collected Verses Vol. 2 (*Hale*)
News of the World (*Scottish Cultural Press*)

The Burns Encyclopedia (*Hale*)
The Castles of Scotland (*Constable*)

With Joyce Lindsay

The Theatre and Opera-lovers' Quotation Book (*Hale*)
The Music-Lovers' Quotation Book (*Hale*)
The Scottish Quotation Book (*Hale*)

Poetry from Scottish Cultural Press
For a complete listing of poetry currently available from Scottish Cultural Press, including the *Scottish Contemporary Poets* series, please contact the publishers direct.

SPEAKING LIKENESSES

A Postscript

Maurice Lindsay

SCOTTISH CULTURAL PRESS
Edinburgh

First published 1997
Scottish Cultural Press
Unit 14, Leith Walk Business Centre, 130 Leith Walk
Edinburgh EH6 5DT
Tel: 0131 555 5950 • Fax: 0131 555 5018

British Library Cataloguing in Publication Data
A catalogue record for this book is available from the British Library

ISBN: 1 898218 96 X

Printed and bound by
Cromwell Press, Melksham

CONTENTS

...and Lighter Verses

Maurice Lindsay

Well known as poet, writer, critic and broadcaster, Maurice Lindsay was born in Glasgow in 1918. Educated at Glasgow Academy, he was the first boy in the school to take Higher Music; an accident to his wrist, however, put an end to any prospect of a musical career. Commissioned in the Cameronians shortly before war broke out, he latterly served as a Staff officer in the War Office. Music critic of *The Bulletin* for 14 years, he became Programme Controller for the new Border TV in 1961, and the first Director of The Scottish Civic Trust in 1967. From 1983-90 he was Hon.Sec. General of Europa Nostra. Some of his other works include the 2-volume *The Lowlands of Scotland*; *Robert Burns: the Man, the Work, the Legend*; *The Burns Encyclopedia*; *The Castles of Scotland*; *Collected Poems 1940-90*; *On the Face of It:Collected Poems Vol. 2*; and *News of the World.* With his wife, Joyce, he has edited several books of quotations, including the best-selling *Music Quotation Book.*

Accused by some of ignoring 'modernism' and 'post-modernism' in poetry, Maurice Lindsay comments: 'I write about what moves or angers me and as I please. The purpose of poetry should aim to provide pleasure for ordinary people, not teaching fodder for trendy academics

PREFACE

When *News of the World* was published (Scottish Cultural Press, 1995) I subtitled it *Last Poems*. Most elderly poets – and many younger – believe that each newly-completed poem may turn out to be their last. To my surprise, I found that over a period of twenty months in 1994-96 I experienced quite a flow of poems. As Kenneth Roy, introducing three of these new poems in the *Scottish Review*, No. 6, put it: "He said he would write no more, but the poems kept coming." One cannot have a "laster poems", so I am bound to emulate the last of the great theatrical actor-managers, Sir John Martin-Harvey, whose "final" appearances were followed by "farewell" and "definitely farewell" appearances; although this time I really do believe *Speaking Likenesses* is a "last poems" volume. This publication will, I hope, mark my eightieth year. I trust that my daughter, Mrs Kirsteen Stokes, in conjunction with the scholar and critic Dr Carol Gow, may in due course bring out *Complete Poems*, mainly containing *Collected Poems 1940-1990*, the volumes published since its appearance, of which this is the third and whatever else they think merits preservation.

The book falls into two sections, though not so delineated: serious poems and lighter verse, which I have always enjoyed writing, believing that, as with legendary heaven, poetry has many mansions.

Some of these poems made their first appearance in *Chapman*, *The Herald*, *Interim* (USA), *Lines Review*, *North Words*, *The Scots Magazine*, *Scottish Review*, *Skinklin Star* and *West Coast Magazine*. "Voyages" was written for the festschrift presented to the Literary Director of the Scottish Arts Council, Mr Walter Cairns, on his retirement in April 1996. The Norman MacCaig "Birthday Card" was written for a little collection produced by Joy Hendry, the Editor of *Chapman*, to mark that poet's eighty-fifth birthday.

Some Georgian poet or other – I forget which – once asked, rhetorically: "Where does the uttered music go?" The same place as the uttered radio or television programme, presumably. In the first of the BBC television comedy series *Waiting for God*, Diana, the acerbic character played by Stephanie Cole, on being accused of "lack of faith" by her companion, Tom, burst out with the wonderful retort: "Faith is the quantum leap to the bloody ridiculous". I thought it a pity that so witty an aphorism should go the way of the uttered music, so I therefore adapted it slightly to become the last line of my sonnet "A Humanist".

I am indebted to my wife, Joyce, and to my secretary, Mrs Joan Cunningham, for patiently word-processing the various versions through which these poems have gone before reaching final form.

Maurice Lindsay

To my friend and fellow poet James Aitchison,
without whose critical encouragement
there would have been no Postscript.

Voyages
(for Walter Cairns)

There were always voyages to look forward to –
an uncle's plowtered dinghy across the pond
in Great Western Road, where water plashed the oars
with dripping colours; and, darting nimbly around,
minnows, grey as the water's muddy ground.

Later, a horse-drawn cab to the Broomielaw,
embarked from to sail across the great divide
that summered freedom: Innellan, a paradise
of childhood; small crabs scuttling away to hide
in rocky shadows; the bracing swim of the Clyde;

or cruising afternoon islands, mountainy lochs –
the phut-phut paddles, the rising and falling thrust
of the engines; the heated smell of used-up oil;
the number of steamers we'd managed to sail on discussed
as we chewed our fresh-air hunger crisp to the crust:

or sculling a boat at night with trailing lines
of anticipation out to the Gantock rocks,
where a flash of mackerel slivered the water's thresh
as we hauled them in, gave their heads a couple of socks
on the gunnel, the floor a twitch of head–tail knocks.

Later, my annual trip to the Orkney Isles
on the *Earl Rognvald**, a vessel so toughly old
pulled by the tugging strains of the Pentland Firth,
I'd smell the cattle for fattening sick in the hold,
while two seas thumped her hull as she pitched and rolled.

Then there were crossings to Ireland, where once my folk
struggled to weed their patch of old bigotries
by the shores of Lough Swilly: trapped by angered law,
they fled intolerance, the religious disease
of ignorance no reason can ever appease.

*pronounced *Ronald*

1

Later still, with the luggage of middle age,
on island-bagging liners, a warmer ocean;
excursioned facts, sales-touted souvenirs;
the throb of the screw and the gently-shuddered motion
creaking her decks as she prowed the sea's commotion.

On the stately Rhine and Danube rivers, where ruined
castles once threw strategic gauntlets down,
deck-chaired passenger-barges struggle against
the current racing beneath dead history's frown
that wind and rain have rinsed clean to the bone.

New Orleans, swanning the full-brimmed Mississippi,
where last-stand British red-coats were forced to yield,
on a rear-wheeled replica such as Southern masters
once sailed through slaving cotton, field after field,
harvesting racial hate that has never healed.

Now, in a house first built by an old sea-captain
who wanted to feel that he still gazed out from his bridge
I watch the little waves of an estuary
draw themselves up, unroll; each glassy ridge
sun-semaphoring summer's privilege

and think how, rusting here in a laid-up berth,
(though questing eddies linger my last retreat)
the meaning's never where you set out to explore it;
through whatever seas, the soundings are incomplete –
it's the tide of life itself that keeps running sweet.

A Birthday Card for Norman MacCaig at Eighty-Five

Birds, fishermen and boats; a mountain's language;
the unpersuadable accents of the sea;
collies; old women; requiems of anguish;
acceptance edged with life's expectancy
in words clear as the breathing winds' keaning
tuned to fresh imagery at every touch.
Honour to one who new-dimensioned meaning
with wonder and delight; and gave so much.

The Anti-Foodie

*Unlike you, I eat to live, not live
to eat*, the little executive sauced out of the room,
well-satisfied that he'd been able to give
his cap of argument a kind of plume.

I thought of how he strove to advance his rank,
the effort wizening his worried brow;
and how, with his superiors, he drank
only pure water, since he couldn't allow

indulgence flavour Calvin's witnessed creed –
unlike the French, whose cooking was, he'd claim,
the elevation of our animal need
into a sensual time-consuming game!

I thought of the things that mattered most in life –
good health and music; books and plays; great art,
but, above all, a warmly-loving wife,
and children of whom both of you are part,

sitting around the table at their food,
their appetites maturing from shrill cries
of: *Must I eat this? It isn't any good!*
to: *Mum, that's wizzo. What a great surprise!*

And, as the world upon their shoulders turns –
their palates, sharpened with the critic's tool,
comparison – as haggis was to Burns,
delight in what they like becomes the rule.

O little men for whom the yielding feel
of human pleasure's weakness to deplore –
oysters, oatcakes and salmon for a meal,
I'll down you in a pledge of smooth Bowmore!

In the Kitchen

First, there's the laying out; ingredients
well-quantified, conveniently to hand.
Then next the preparation; pungent scents;
cut parsley, scraping carrots, peeled-off strand
of onions, watering eyes with glistening skin.
Finally, cooking; fish or meat prepared
with herb and seasoning, then put quickly in
the oven's grasp, caressing flavours shared.
A change from crafting poems, cooking food! –
poems that only other poets read,
stirring reviewers' bile through what tastes good.
Steam-trembled lids of pots recite a need
all human hunger anciently commands,
and satisfaction feeds with timeless hands.

Values

We are a dying race, we printed poets,
too much concerned with formal things, while fate
keeps forcing life through gullies of disaster,
leaving *too little* stranded on *too late*;
man's inhumanity to man deplored
refuged in noisy news sheets' rival greeds,
where politicians salvo pointless words
that pity cannot hear and no one heeds.

Poets in pubs are now the verbal masters
who celebrate the vagaries of luck;
the loudly-sweating moment's brief employment –
the one-night stand, the underhanding buck –
with words that rinse like froth from dirty glasses
reshelved; poured with tomorrow's quick enjoyment;
lines that fill out some bustle's brittle pause,
a here-and-now untouched by time or cause.

4

On Declining to Write an Obituary

What happens when ambition drives to the end
of the road and a blind sign utters NO ADMITTANCE?
Grudge life out with a disappointee's quittance?
Or leave the forgotten block behind and bend
first purposes to where there's an open way,
a new direction, mapping different signs
for wonder to follow, eagerness obey?
One who fumed on irreversible lines
let indignation steam his halted stay,
though travelled further than merit seemed to fuel
thought he should reach beyond and sought to prolong
his sense of static failure with a cruel
self-righteousness, ridging a humourless pose
that looked down loftily on lesser folk,
thanking blamed God he wasn't one of those
who felt the sting of each sardonic joke
avenged upon the world that did him wrong.

As we all must, the other day he died
and while awaiting burial he lay,
no prattled child or fellow-traveller cried;
for one who, somehow, swamped beside the way
obiturists found no lost words to say.

Black Shoulderbeast

I remember the tree-lined tramcar-clanging road
by the Botanic Gardens, and the church
where I was sent to gloom with Scotland's God,
who left me in the disbelievers' lurch;

a lonely boy walking by stiff-ranked flowers,
contrasting green-strip lengths of new-mown lawns;
nursemaids wheeling their charges' fresh-air hours,
with rustling starchy gossip sit-upons

lining the benches as I wandered by
clutching a book of poems and wondering how
and when I'd write my own, yet somewhere try
to gear myself into the here-and-now-

world, busily shifting everyone but me
about some monied purpose. Time seemed long,
and surely in the years ahead I'd see
ambition look my way and I'd belong?

Sixty years on, I limp the self-same gardens,
gossiping nursemaids and their charges gone,
ambition's youthful fret the stuff that hardens
the veins of resignation. Suns that shone
the seeming promise of applauded day
now set upon a footnote also-ran,
obliterating all he strove to say,
the lines erased before the breathing man.

Fifty Years On

Will it be so again?[1] the poet asked
and answered: *It will not be so again.*
Yet he was wrong, that gentle Irish bard:
war's refugees still stream the dying plain;
flee human wretchedness, once more unmasked
as pitiless greed outflanks frail reason's guard
and might takes up its ancient killing game.
It was ever thus. Must it always be so again?

[1]Cecil Day Lewis

Our Times: An Epitaph

She thought her parents fussy, old and square;
upholders of establishment convention
who criticised the clothes she liked to wear,
saucing her out the room whenever mention
of drugs, or drink, or unprotected sex
was focused through some media report.
Nothing to do with her; just said to vex.
Disaster was a fate she wouldn't court!
Only young once, she argued, pleasures must
be seized where they are offered; and besides,
most blokes are decent if you show them trust,
late dancing, friendly drinking, thumbing rides.
They found her naked, strangled in a ditch:
the avid readers muttering: *Silly bitch!*

Crime Passionnel

He bloated swagger, reputation's bully,
spitting out sallow oaths. When puberty
seized him, he leered his level best to sully
girls who allowed the slightest liberty.
One awed child-bride assumed that she could tame him,
haltered in marriage. High in minded will,
she scolded whoring, drink and drugs to shame him,
not sensing when he lusted for the kill.
Fresh from the latest fascinated filly
he'd wrenched from her virginity, his wife –
one drunken, battered night he'd fucked her silly –
ripped the beat of his heart with a carving knife;
cutting through civilisation's thin veneer,
the hunter's forest and the hungry snare.

Parties

Parties, meant to be fun for all, for one boy
rarely ever were. The kind where horse-drawn
cabs arrived outside the door of Winter;
the waiting horse's visible breath, the cabby
flapping his arms against his greenish coat
as we came shimmering down in party clothes
climbing our stepping-stone to the musty smell
well-boxed inside. Or children come to our house,
sitting on benches shy against the wall,
boys printing oily hair-marks that annoyed
my mother; playing *Dree-a-dree-I dropped-it*
or *Ring-a-ring-of-roses* till excitements
made adults organise *Dead Animals*.

Later, a smooth white ball-cloth stretched across
the drawing-room carpet; awkward teen-age dancing;
embarrassment with sandwiches and cakes.

I passed the house the other day, divided
now into flats, the sweetly-smelling stables
that later fumed with hired-out limousines
a supermarket. There, I memoried,
aisled with young mothers trailing *I want* children
filling up routine trollies.

　　　　　　　　　"Watch that old man's sticks,"
one chatting mother raucoused. *Quite all right*,
I said, aware their commonality
of daily-shared concerns, the harassed strains
of domesticity, must make me seem
an oddity; some left-behind old party
after go-home time no one had collected.

Street Sounds

When I was young pavemented Sunday mornings
clangoured with bells. Dark-suited people came,
clutching black bibles, through the summoned warning
that those who stayed away were clothed in blame
and somehow laxed more easily in sin
(the Devil everywhere a long-armed reacher)
while, sore on boring wooden pews, we'd win
protective wisdom droned out by the preacher.

Weekday bells sang out more cheerfully:
for brides with lacery billowed on the breeze;
for royal birthdays, fancied victories;
for public gratitude or practised ease.
Now that no longer Sunday-best good people
believe in silent myth-vacated Heaven,
or answer to the fretted call of steeple,
or think that sin exists to be forgiven,

alarm's what amplifies its passage-way
for ambulances paced by pawing death;
a wail of police to accident or affray;
fire-engine clanged to douse the black-faced breath
of choking flames. We pull aside, let pass
the destination of whatever threat
finds others, thankful that it wasn't us;
move on and let normality forget.

Bland tourists, we still pay our casual fee
where great cathedrals shrug their vanished cause
around a faithful praying coterie;
while, now and then, a shower of pealing awes
us, like some old castle firing blanks,
saluting earthly honours in defiance
of lost magnificence that once gave thanks
for Church and State unbreached in grim alliance.

Now, what assails our ears is neither glory
nor grandeur draped in falsified illusion,
but wounded human bodies; broken, gory
with violence, or frightened in confusion.
Better to hear of tolled mortality

from sounds that rush to succour such distress
than worship gods of unreality
or prophets who intolerantly bless!

The Leven at Dumbarton

Slipping their rushy sedge, the swans glide
from loch to river; past small anchored boats
twice-daily turning sterns against the tide.
Indifferent, the white flotilla floats,
not part of our world. Yet their cold concerns
relax as little boys break crusts of bread
and toss them through the railings. Water churns
as webbed feet paddle faster towards the spread
of bobbing scraps. Held dignity forgot,
unquestioned necks reach down to beak a share,
jostling till not a morsel's to be got,
the paper bags are litter, crumpled air,
dropped as the boys chase laughter through the street,
leaving the swans regroup their silent fleet.

Summer Park

The boating-pond keeps bending trees and bushes
over a rippled upward-looking sky.
Out from the bank a shining small boy pushes
an electronic liner. His ally,
grasping the ghost of childhood in his hands,
twists the remote controls. The liner sails
round hectic circles. Smiling, father stands,
lost in the happy shouts the voyage hails.
Then small boy loses interest, wanting sweets,
time still too short for satisfaction's measures,
anticipation eagering fresh treats,
not knowing what lost dream his father treasures,
steering the boat to shore, wiping it dry,
re-boxing wonder trailed from years long by.

Summer Fountain

Behind a discreet dustily-coated bush
some park attendant turned on a brass tap.
Silence got taken over by a *whoosh*
that settled to a *hiss* as, from its lap,
the water opened up a parasol
of coloured iridescence round the heads
of chipped gilt angels centering the bowl
of the marble fountain; spittering nearby beds
of gaudily-marshalled municipal flowers.

Mothers strolling with children traced their *oohs*!
while men who walked through lives of workless hours,
sloughing off time that boredom hoped to lose,
looked round to see this rain, like crystal hair
curving a dotted arch against the sun;
a limpid, moveless, motion, hung on air,
whose held delight defied comparison.

Summer Bandstand

They came on Friday afternoons to hear
the band; a kind of municipal treat;
the military uniforms up there
brassily blaring: the staccato beat

of their conducting major, brisk command
to blow in step and keep the music moving,
not letting softer feelings countermand
the martial red-coat pace with unimproving

sentiment, such as listening nursemaids knew,
rocking the handles of expensive prams;
the pleasure that must one day be their due
as surely as it once had been "Madam's".

11

About their knees the older children play,
bored with uncomprehended artifice,
forever girning: *What's the time of day?*
or: *How much longer must we sit through this?*

Meanwhile, old rheumy men, chins propped on sticks,
wince when the toddlers pierce a sudden jag
of screamed frustration that the nursemaids fix.
Soft breezes flap the music like a flag...

Retracing distance seven decades on,
there's now an open clearing; Gothic twirls
of iron bandstand and its seating, gone;
an emptiness which only winter swirls.

The Woods of Auchentorlie

With V-shaped face that mocks solemnity
an owl sits hatching silence in its tree,
till darkness draws down anonymity
over the shapes of daylight; flits, *tu-wits,*
tu-woos, but mostly sits and glares,
piercing the veiled protection as it stares
out subtleties of movement we can't see;
waiting for mice, or shrews, or voles
to scutter from their furried holes,
then pause to listen if some creaking might
pose menace through the blackened symmetry.

Noiseless in soft-plumed flight
the owl plunges, undercarriaged claws
lowered to tear a small cry out of night,
then, scooping back its warm light-bloodied prey,
gorges; flits through its shadows, sits to await
sleep as the blundered world resumes its way,
unsheathing wars for this or that lost cause,
killing when there's no appetite to sate.

Late Autumn Morning, Milton Hill

A lapping mist along the riverside
had licked the openness of light away,
leaving behind discarded urban breath
rising across the water, white-ish grey;
blinding the routine motorists, turning back
their groping headlights to a yellowed glare
that lurked – however much they frowned and peered –
half-muffled danger shaping everywhere.
As if a disconnected cloud had dropped
round Milton Hill, blue sunshine coldly shone
across an undulating fleecy drape,
such as air travellers look down upon;

spreading suspended silence, through which droned
the growl of revving engines: warp and woof
of business, news and politics, from which,
briefly, primeval dawn remained aloof.

Milton Hill, Mid-Winter

As if some soothing hush was being sprinkled
out of a greyly-pouching gathered sky,
the first flakes disappeared, alighting gently,
wetting the road. *Do you think it's going to lie?*

we ask ourselves, as muffled flakes keep sifting
over the peering misted window-pane,
blurring out edges, levelling fields and furring
the trees ripped black by winter. Thick with strain,

the piled-up burden bends the resting sap
till branches shake loose shivers to the ground.
Skin-crinkled cold, the air appears to shrink
in quietness; until the coughing sound

the gritter's lorry grumbles up the hill
with, loudens keen-eared distance, listening
as silent stealthy-footed darkness locks
on frost, fastening tight its fix of glistening.

Snow falls on staring, sheeted snow; then whisks,
as if some passing wind's invisible feather
frothed up impassable drifts on country roads.
Colder, we say. *We're in for heavy weather.*

Over the Bridge

I look down over the bridge of years and stare
through shadows that declaim a waterfall
narrowed by rocks it curtains. Chattering where
motion and stillness seem equivocal
lie two small boys, their careful shirt-sleeves rolled
although half-drenched by mists of tumbled spray,
arming excuse that mothers wouldn't scold,
trailing loose eddies spun from the affray.
And I remember how I, too, one day
felt idly-drifting fingers half-resist
the pull of waters long since flowed away,
rippling the pillars of my guddled wrists,
to reach the ever-nearing level sea
of washed-up human possibility.

On the Beach At Helensburgh

My dogs splosh with enjoyment, dripping sea
from chased-for sticks, till one of them alerts
the other to the wrack flung up the beach,
raised by the arms of Winter. Scent diverts
retrieving concentration. Dry dulse crumbles
as paws, scraping excitement, first uncover

plastic gone shapeless; tins rough-edged with rust;
a condom worn by some discarded lover;

then, tashed beneath, a seabird's body, ringed
with scarlet plastic round one yellow foot –
white-feathered energy now dulled and stilled
beyond the raging elements' dispute

it met flick-eyed. What dropped its final flight,
and wrought destruction on its aimless travel,
the flapping winds have spread their wings upon.

This broken smell of death and salty gravel
soon bores the dogs. Chasing their chewed-up sticks
proves better fun than nosing fallen bones
that air abandoned, leaving earth to moulder
decay's routine which eager life disowns
and dogs and seabirds never have to ponder.

Revisiting the West Bay, Dunoon: 1995

Varnish-gleaming dinghies leant on their sides
in drawn-up groups along the curve of the bay,
beneath white huts, beyond the grasp of the tides.
Watching the glint of Summers wear away,
old clay-piped sea-dogs, squinting sailor-caps,
hired hourly rows for amateurs by day,
sweeping a wary eye for such mishaps
as drifted oars or rowlocks dropped in the bay.
We regulars, at dusk, pulled out for The Gantocks,
trailing our lines for mackerel; plashing drips
of phosphorescent green as, round the rocks
we flapped them in – twenty or so on trips
lasting two darkened hours. Then home, content
with shouldered strung-up catch, to cool-sheet bed,
awakened by the rising breakfast scent
of frying mackerel and fresh-baked bread.

Near seventy years have passed; that eager edge
of living's blunted; huts and boats are gone;
the sharp-tailed mackerel's the privilege
of quotas, trawling nets so preyed-upon
as threatened its extinction. Up the beach
only the waves still voice their empty reach.

Filming Iona

It slides from under vapoured cloud; a splodge
of greenness shallowed in a sandy sea.
Our shadowed helicopter-blades dislodge
opened reflections on its surface. We
climb out our cockpit, handing down the gear
to capture it on footage for TV;
filming half legend, half an atmosphere,
grave mythological kings, a Saint's decree
that winds of doubting centuries have blown
away and can't, unlike the abbey stones,
be lovingly restored – they're not what's shown,
but images that agelessness enthrones:
light etching sea on shore; a timeless creed
still there to soothe unpraying human need.

Loch Ossian

Cocked on the roof of Scotland, compass eye
gazing a stretch of sky that stares it back;
glimpsed-at by passing trains; a Summer's rest
for tired hill-walkers, setting down their packs
to slake clear water, lave their climbed-out limbs
with momentary rest beside a shore
where eagles trail their shadowed flight: all else
bare legend stripped by naked Winter's roar.

Worlds Apart

Walking the dog at Overtoun one day,
hard by the rushes round the lily-pond,
slap in the middle of our grassy way,
a blown-up marsh-edge bubbled vagabond
squatted, broad-angled head held high; splayed feet;
mottled in greens – a kind of breathing stare:
not what a snuffled dog expects to meet
furred from the grass and bracken growing there.
Braked paws, cocked ears, head questioned side-to-side,
the dog stared at the toad, frightened to pass;
till the thing sprang the narrow safe divide
between it and the pond. Into long grass
the trembling dog went plunging; then emerged
bright-eyed, unshivered, shameful terror purged.

Greyhound

He'd covered years of distance, winning races
that often breasted home the fleeted gains
of betting, pounding round those breathless lanes
where other greyhounds strained for faster paces;
was roughly fondled down his narrow ears,
not with affection, but because each prize
made him in his beloved owner's eyes
a cause for boasting over paid-for beers.
Until, one day, electric hares moved faster
than heart and legs could gain upon. Out running
beside the town's canal, picked up and thrown
into the water by his worshipped master
and held beneath with struggled senses stunning,
a jogger hearing: *Drown, you bastard, drown.*

17

i
Country Laird

Where d'y winter? my dinner-neighbour barked,
red-faced, as if a serious accusation
was being levelled, I not having marked
some obsequy that mourned a grieving nation:
"We own two basset-hounds, so aren't able
to be away long periods." *My hounds,*
I'd have you know, stand belly-high with the table,
he snarled, as if the next word might be zounds:
My factor doesn't feel the bloody cold
so I go after sunshine; somewhere near a
casino, where they pamper you when old;
like Marakesh, Bermuda or Madeira.
A chilling man, alone and winter-hearted,
arriving long before he had departed.

ii
Lady of the House

Ill-at-ease with herself, begrudging life
that somehow stole an unfair march on her,
this pampered daughter, half a grown-up wife,
thought that her husband's riches cast a slur
on her pretensions, for he sold wholesale
condoms that levelled poor men, crooks and kings,
yet couldn't talk you up the social scale,
however much they raised up other things.
Not even whopping diamonds, shouting gleams
less-bosomed women envied, brought relief.
Though pleasure's rarely where or why it seems,
dissatisfaction plays the double thief
since boredom, stretching triviality's length
itself becomes a kind of inner strength.

iii
Far Left of Centre

He was born objecting. Nurtured in the wrong,
a skill he'd mastered with the facts of school –
false teaching bent to benefit the strong –
shunning him on the lone side of each rule
the others crowded with acceptance. Age
smoothed him to clichés that could sound a throng
to swelling protest. On life's daily page,
turned casually, his name did not belong.
Whenever he voiced indignant shadows, shouting
the odds on equal rights for Everyman,
self-interests quickly organised his routing.
What made him think a writ for weakness ran,
however conscience twinged pretended care,
a world swirling in chance be somehow fair?

iv
Astrologer

At first he treated it as a well-paid joke,
scanning the sky to fake-up fortune-telling,
although he'd always been the first to poke
fun at all supernatural merchants, selling
fables they'd not experienced. Pretence,
fine-honed, becomes unshakeable belief,
ghosts, gods and futures read like seeming sense
when simple folk achieve some chance relief.
A round of hours was all he prophesised
not after-life eternity, like priests –
his pseudo-truths a night's good sleep denied;
besides which, only brains the least of leasts
would think that stars light-million years away
could zodiac one brief collective day!

v

Terrorist

It was God Himself who told me to do it! "Look,"
He said: "You're the one I've picked to avenge my Cause.
Too bad if the innocent perish. Bring to book
as many as you can. They've broken my laws
by slighting you, my elected agent, sent
to show my strength and to give the sick world pause
that's turned against you as I never meant
it to, the dark side of my crucified son!"
To disobey such a call would be mortal sin
so I hoarded obedient weapons to wait the chance
when enough would be gathered together for such a win
as would show His certainty of circumstance.
Ears bursting with the loud voice of His will,
I triggered random aim as he shouted: "Kill!"

vi

Humanist

What sort of God, the wary philosopher mused,
possesses absolute omnipotence
and yet lets innocent children be abused;
suffers in prayerful silence the immense
obscenities of escalating war
that multiplies its killing power; seas
whipped into drowning hurricanes; the jar
of grinding plates beneath the soil that shock
erupting earthquakes, scattering devastation?
What caused the uncaused cause to wind the clock
of life up? Each religious explanation
depends on faith in man-made dogma's truss:
a quantum leap to the ridiculous!

vii
Speaking Likenesses

He read my portrait of him; bumbling Tom,
carnaptious, kindly, with "a heart of gold",
Bang on, he'd say with glee: *went like a bomb!*
his clichés turning thought round every fold;
worth more than birds in bushes; and no bones
to deepen dark in which all cats are grey,
or gather doubting moss on rolling stones,
the slate wiped clean with every dawning day.
Clean as a whistle, with so thick a skin
no stitch in time was ever made too soon,
since being one of those who couldn't win,
cat out of bag, then up went some balloon.
Over his face I watched slow pleasure spill.
My God! The speaking likeness of old Bill!

viii
Patient

"You're looking well today," said one old fellow,
greeting his friend. *Appearances deceive*,
the other answered. *See, my eyeball's yellow*,
pulling down pouching shadows. *I receive
treatment for asthma, boils, a dicky heart;
and trouble's blueing in my varicose veins.
The doctor hints I'm acting out a part,
imagining my range of aches and pains.
At night, I lightly sleep an hour or two,
yet all he ever does is hum and fudge,
as if I were some fake that he'd seen through:
since it's my body, I'm the better judge.
But I'm not bashful; always speak my mind:
it's strange how doctoring skills have so declined!*

ix
Dunroamin

She'd bought the obvious souvenirs everywhere:
a wooden wind-mill, strung-up china clogs
from Holland; a green-ribboned pair
of black shillelaghs, smoothed from Ireland's bogs;
a tartan terrier; silver-peaked hinged lid
South German beer mug; London policeman's helmet,
toy bus; Swiss cuckoo-clock; in frozen bid,
escaped Murano sea-birds glassed her pelmet.
My, she's well-travelled, neighbours used to say,
watching the Alpine hut where figures swung –
he, out for rain; she, on a sunny day –
God Bless This House, her cross-framed motto hung.
Were He up there, indeed, He surely might,
for so much tasteless innocent delight!

x
Cornered

A daily fixture at a far-back desk
of the Library Reading Room; glazed mackintosh
kept on; lank-haired, unshavenly grotesque,
eye-shunned when noticed by the brusquely posh
researchers after business reference;
vacantly stared-at with unseeing glance –
books scattered open, sucking thoughtful pens –
by students in their memorizing trance.
He plucked newspapers dressed in wooden spines
down, one by one, and studied every page,
stubbed finger searched across the printed lines
that neither news nor knowledge could assuage:
all that he sought-for from his life's defeat,
eight free short rainless hours of civic heat.

xi
Photograph

I look back at myself in uniform,
cane under arm, tunic and tartan trews
immaculate, half-sitting on that edge
of confidence authority endues;
young officer, a rookie in disguise,
uncertain what it was he could command,
bring order to the gap from *then* to *now*;
how little he would ever understand
of life's defaulting. Acres of the heart
lay unexplored behind that photo-smile
happiness, satisfactions, failures, halts
that tolerant age has learnt to reconcile.
As wonder cadences its dying fall
old photograph, I turn you to the wall.

xii
Visitation

Easing himself inside her parlour door,
the bleakly Reverend Habakkuk MacQueen –
as oozily a pious wordy bore
as ever dog had collared – came between
Jemima Smith and tough red-headed Willie,
her only son, impatiently sixteen,
promised a bike if he said nothing silly
until the Man of God had safely been.
A little sherry? "I don't drink strong liquor."
Perhaps some soup? "No, calories make one fat."
Some meat, then? "Eating corpses makes me sick;
feel guilty." On his fidget Willie sat:
"Mother, sin ye've gat naethin that he'd like,
bile the auld fule an egg and tae hell wi ma bike!"

xiii
Casino

A daze of blue beneath green-shaded light
hovers the gaming tables, round which crouch
ancient white staring faces. Bodiced tight
above smoothed elegant drapes, the loud breasts pouch
their cleavage as the croupiers' wooden rakes
lean to claw in the takings. Veined hands, fat
with rings, count chips while mouthing odds-on-stakes,
half-glancing what their fingers fumble at.
Inhaling cigarettes, as if dear life
depended on it, some compulsive grip
untensions boredom from the widowed wife,
gives roués' shadowed aimlessness the slip
seized by the suppuration of mad chance
that only death or poverty could lance.

xiv
Old Age

Whenever he settled into a comfy chair,
purposing tides receded, leaving him
stranded upon inaction: unaware
of what his energies had planned to limn
upon the canvas of another day –
so great a space of interest to fill
accomplishment with, his mind in eager play –
intentions lapped-on by his drowsy will;
waters that rinsed away the recent names
he'd processed in the internet of years
his memory computered; playing games,
recalling those where distance most adheres.
What have I missed? some twinged arthritic ache
refloated him, unmoored and half-awake

Dilemma

A green and yellow wriggle, multi-tread,
a shrugging line of shoulders as it heaves
laborious twistings down thin stems, to leaves
it laces ragged holes in where it fed.

Roses, nasturtiums, marigolds and trees
fruiting for Autumn its especial taste;
textures and linking veins alike laid waste –
whatever's green its pinpoint searching sees.

"Insects are part of Nature's how and why;
we must respect them," conservationists say.
"A pity to deny one fluttered day
an opened pupa claims as butterfly."
But conservation has to be two-way,
he harumphed as he pressed his can of spray.

A Calling Card

Allow me to introduce myself. I'm God's
unpleasant side; like Him, by you created
to even up, I'd guess, the boring odds
goodness and pleasured ease might leave you sated.
I'm black-as-painted; coin's reverse; hid moon
as earth spins doubly round its axis pole –
midnight for others while for some, high noon –
the conscience pricking your imagined soul:
the heart of what my opposite gave you; choice
to torture, cheat, make wars with fractured laws;
like Him, a silent fancied inner voice,
though I don't seek perpetual applause.
What you are here for, where faith claims you'll go,
how in the name of Hell am I to know?

Kissing Earth

The Pope, that ancient celibate,
seems strangely sure of women's needs,
losing no chance to preach and prate
unfettered married sex that breeds.
No matter how we cultivate
blind faith, it's tending fertile seeds
with husbandry to generate
what triumphs over fertile weeds
keeps piety in pomp and state
to spider monkish man-made creeds
with fancied after-life for bait.
Unstarving death is all he feeds.

A Question of Theology

Some fifteen thousand million years, he said
have passed since some explosion rocked the universe,
What happened wrong side of the watershed
that turned BC AD? Did God rehearse
redemption, letting brutish ape-man flourish
millennia before some cold extinction
removed his kind? That failure used to cherish
our sort of super-animal distinction?
Is cosy Heaven bright-attiring priests
proclaiming Hell a centre brimmed with smells
of burning, cultured heathen, upright beasts –
whatever wound-back evolution swells?
Souldom the saving privilege of the few
fashioned a mere two-thousand seasons new?

Of Miracles

You have to accept the package, the man said,
as he genuflected towards his crucifix;
the certainty of an afterlife when dead;
the virgin birth; the seeming unlikely fix
of immaculate conception and resurrection;
the miracles by which both were brought about –
there isn't room for reason's circumspection
opening cracks in faith for the frosts of doubt.
Once, I believed heaven's voice collided thunder
before I knew each effect must have its cause:
which still leaves room in the universe for wonder
that science can't contain in its proven laws.
Yet whenever rival superstitions get stirred,
gospelling gods, like genii, raise the absurd.

Encountered Credos

What's one in your position, the cleric asked,
to look forward to? It seems to me you've missed
out on all hope of immortality, masked
half-way agnostic, half-way atheist,
blind to the promise Jesus makes complete?
"I believe in the warmth of dailiness," I replied;
"in voices overheard on the casual street;
in different-facing travellers who ride
their journeyed thoughts in silence to defeat;
music, imagination's farthest skills;
poetry shouldered boredom can't unseat;
whatever secular ecstasy distils;
where goodness for a human while prevails:
not in religion's warring fairy-tales!"

The Light of Reason

What is the point of life, the man asked,
without religion?, (not expecting answers);
scraping a meagre living, endlessly tasked
with drugs and booze; forgetful, false enhancers?
The smell of glint-ploughed earth after fresh rain;
the fires of touching flesh; warm-embered age;
the whispered long-eared *whush* of fields of grain;
the search for truth and the wit keen minds engage.
No genuflecting dogma's benedicts
can justify what's rare in its own right,
nor cabin love with supernatural tricks
to make exuberance shameful, joy contrite.
No righting judgement laves celestial light:
but, as before our birth, unknowing night.

The New Map

I

Where did you say you had to go to? Hell.
Just carry straight on down the road. Keep turning
right as often as you can. Easy to find
because the route is paved with good intentions.

What's not so easy's knowing you've arrived there.
A recent group of season-travelled priests
has changed the map. The lake of burning pitch
has been filled in with ready platitudes;
the forking fiery devils made redundant.
Instead of everlasting pain, soft-speakers –
the latest in technology – *sotto voce,*
through virtual reality, keep uttering
chewed sound-bites, used by time-worn politicians,
with both-way-facing double-tonguing words
and sleazy dogma grammared out of greed.

28

II

After some time, they say, you pay no heed
to those grown fat upon the blood of need,
because Hell's climate, so the travellers claim
is negative non-being, lacking name.
Cartographers of piety presume
that somewhere near must be a smaller room;
next door, perhaps: Heaven's sound-proof insulation
where God and His Elect hold conversation ...
How strongly clings the sanctimonious smell
of those who peddle souls to Heaven or Hell!

Outside

Two thousand years these manger walls have stood
sheltering myth – a virgin with her child,
redeeming heaven's legendary good
the robes and riches of the world defiled.
Today, it's unbelief we celebrate
through electronic tills, stale carols blaring
and news of wars that human blood can't sate;
the God-forsaken eyes of hunger staring.
Exporting death, (though calling it "defence"),
we revel in the christmas-cracker glow;
like Santa Claus, an innocent pretence
we hide behind – the yearly goodwill show.
Meanwhile, outside cracked walls, grim shadows wait
nursing some bundled fundamentalist hate.

A Choice of Subject

Why do you keep on harping about God?,
the sheltered academic critic said.
He's passé; out-of-fashion; anti-mod:
every intelligent person knows He's dead.
Write about manners, monies, lottery grants;
who sleeps with whom; who's just become unwed;
the drums of Dante; Hannibal's elephants;
anything "with it" – use your bloody head!
Armies thrown against armies pile up slain.
One side has grim, sectarian God's right ear:
the other cleanses ethnically to gain
the left, with which He'll hear them loud and clear.
How dead are Gods when technological skill
keeps causeless causes bettering ways to kill?

Et In Terra Pax

Peacetime, they say, though thirty little wars
thud puffs of death on unprotesting earth,
obscurity small comfort, since the scars
proclaim the basic stuff of human worth,
powered by certainties of mad belief,
marshalling men from lovers' beds to kill,
distributing the privacy of grief
that never rings up PAID on murder's till.
From the crooked timber of humanity
no straight thing can be made, grim Kant declared,
philosophising man's inanity
until at length even reasoning despaired,
uncertain hope (not "sure", as clerics think)
yawned closer to extinction's edgeless brink.

POLITICAL POEMS

i
Progress

Technology's advancement's found the easy
answer – computers, quicker and cheaper than jobs.
Plushed with share options, bosses aren't queasy –
profit the only word that no one fobs
off with sentiment – cutting the work-force down,
increasing unemployment; scarcely a choice
likely to make right-thinking governments frown,
or listen to the public's muddled voice.
One day, three-quarters of the population
found themselves born to idleness; human scrap.
So they factoried war, since multi-annihilation
seemed the only way to narrow the poverty gap.
But so good was computerised nuclear technique
that they did for themselves, and the rest, in less than a week.

ii
A Question of Balance

Trouble with you, Sir Standing Smoothly said,
is the question of balance. You weigh up, vis-à-vis,
both sides of a problem, just like the BBC,
measuring meaningless numbers; anonymous dead
in a righteous war; or the hyped-up misery
a different system of government than our own
finds that it must apply maintaining law
and order, after its ancient well-tried fashion.

Like blowing rubbish, condemnation gets strewn.
Yet it's all a question of balance. You shouldn't draw
emotional conclusions fanned by passion.

You simply don't understand the political facts.
Bombmania's the largest country on earth;
backward, I grant you; yet it already attracts
keen businessmen to profit from its dearth
of present-day life's equipment – guns and tanks;

landmines, of course – everything civilization
requires a country to have to join the ranks
of progress; count as a thoroughly modern nation.

If I were to protest that they starve girl babies
to death, or cut out the tongue of free speech,
firm orders won would suddenly melt to mebbes,
or quickly slip through the diplomatic breach.

Would you be the one to go to the lads and explain why
their armament factory closed without recompense,
that a horde of anonymous natives needn't die?
There are times when the only course is to straddle the fence...

Who said that politics must make moral sense?

iii
Inner City

The poor are poor. One is sorry for them. There it is.
        E.M. Forster (*Howards End*)

Like garbage creviced in a city street
a passing moment, littering The Square
they stretch full-length along a civic seat,
muttering obscenities. Good folk stare,
pretending not to, nostrils vaguely itching
as if abandoned poverty stank the air;
beyond the hike of any journey's hitching,
lost animals without a sheltered lair.
Born into hopelessness, a squalid slum
festered the growing weakness of despair.
School taught them failure, how to be thought dumb
with no place waiting in the world out there.
I quicken pace, like others, hurrying by,
since there, but for a throw of chance, lie I.

iv
Taken Over

Another merger of two giant firms,
the news reports. _Their profits may be doubled._
Thousands of jobs will go. My conscience squirms
uneasily, though it could stay untroubled,
having no shares and being unconcerned
with profits thus acquired by corporate greed,
the leisure of old-age just what I've earned;
but all around me grows cold-shadowed need.
Are idling generations yet unborn
never to know society's employment?
Or find, at forty-five, they've breached the scorn
of ageists, be deprived of life's enjoyment?
The only way, boasts business, _things can go._
I hear the silent future's gathering _No!_

v
Costa del Sol

Under my balcony window, on the beach
yesterday's masters stroll the heavy sand,
those levers of society out of reach
that once they pulled, enabling them command
some movement in the flux and flow that chance
histories life with. Lightly running past
them, children skip their futuristic dance
through hoops of laughter. Trotting briskly, fast-
foot dogs pursue their purposes, paw marks
impressing small abandonment of care
that scraps of chatter and staccato barks
flap holiday on sea-accustomed air.
Meanwhile, the Mediterranean, sucking stones
under its breath, to repossess its shore,
takes back the borrowed pleasuring it loans,
unsurging rubbed-out strength with every roar,
leaving behind a smooth reflecting sheen,
as if those daylight prints had never been.

vi
Europhobe

He pictured himself, like the white cliffs of Dover,
holding back tides that kept on floundering in
foreign corruptions: bureaucrat changing over
the wrong side of the road; half-envied sin
vaguely connected with sex; disgusting food –
frogs' legs and snails – no Englishman would eat;
a Europe anxious to weld some common good,
that nationalistic wars would shrink retreat.
Sovereignty!, he declared: *God save the Queen
and the Anglican Church, Defender of the Faith!*,
unaware the prayer-filled power that once had been
England's was now an imaginary wraith
draped in a flag with colours coming apart
as Scots reclaim Saint Andrew from its heart.

Genius in George Street

An ordinary Festival afternoon;
George Street, with Summer's idling passers-by
window-shopping; behind them, rows of cars
slanted across the crown of the road; a scene
such as the Tourist Board encourages... Suddenly

a slight man wearing an anxious look behind
thick black-rimmed glasses, raincoat flapping free
and black musician's hat, hurries along
the distanced footsteps ghosting Scott and Hogg;
carrying under his arm a paper parcel,
turning into the George Hotel, where tartan-
skirted countesses, dollared tourists and the wives
of Edinburgh's good and great, sit drinking
elegant chatter clinked on cups of tea.

Unnoticed, Shostakovitch glances past them,
taking the lift to his room for a rest before bracing
another cheering audience out of their seats
with his twentieth-century's violence of oppression,

34

symphonying the human spirit's triumph –
all that will live, the breath of history.

He bows from the podium to roaring applause
for what he'd written out of himself hard years
ago in a lonely Soviet room; then shakes
the smiling bow-tapping orchestra-leader's hand.

After a nervous celebrity supper, exchanging
platitudes through an owlish interpreter,
he slips away from the comfortable company
to his hotel where assertive affluent drinkers
fuddle their fluids, exchanging louder trivia.
Passing unnoticed through them, he disappears
behind the anonymous elevator doors,
at home again with his imagination...

Answers and Questions
(Thoughts on the Two Hundredth Anniversary of Burns's death)

They told you once, as a trainee interviewer,
eliciting information the public seeks,
never to joke about people with funny names
like Balls, MacSporran, Macgillicuddy of the Reeks;

never to ask the fellow just fallen down stairs,
breaking both legs and an arm, if it hurts much;
and never let show a slip of your own opinions.
If a politician won't give an answer, then clutch

hard on the question avoided, until he does,
or is seen shiftily not to – the usual case.
It's OK, as a rule, to inquire how it feels
to have heired ten million pounds or won a horse race.

On the whole, though, such a question's unsatisfactory,
inviting a monosyllabic *yup* or *great*;
and there's the limit to a hesitant silence
through which the expectant listener's willing to wait

for a perfectly useless piece of information
that (how can he guess till he hears it?) might make his day.
The truth is, nothing on earth feels like anything else
but however trivial, everything must have its say.

For millions of years this hostile globe kept turning
with nobody aboard to record the facts
of birling space, with its now much sought-for answers;
(there wasn't the need for insecurity pacts).

Yet now that the pinpoint planet's awash with fear
of oblivion; whatever becomes self-aware
must be analysed, measured, cross-referenced, documented...
When the rocks melt with the sun, who's likely to care?

The Class of 'Thirty-Five

So there we were, the class of 'thirty-five,
since then having worn out more than half-a-century;
for the first time since school-days together in one room;
those for the most part lucky to be alive.

I half-remembered the chubby promising faces
bent over papered desks, connecting thought
through concentrating pencils. White-haired, bald
or propping up time on sticks, there still remained traces

of those lost boys – the doctors, generals, judges,
each with distinction honoured about the name
he'd made for himself where youth had blindly chosen –
beneath the slackened benevolence old age fudges
ambition off with. Was it experience gathered
they talked about? The defeats they had picked themselves up
from (as we all must)? The beautiful women wived
to happiness? Pride in successful children fathered?

No. It was when, and how often, some chap was capped
at cricket; who'd bulls-eyed the highest shooting
score; won rugger colours four times over – as if
the years they'd crossed had suddenly been unmapped,

lifting them back to the hopeful road's beginning,
their hills of satisfaction heaved up ahead;
forgetting for a while that at journey's ending
there's little distance left them for restless winning.

The juvenile past they'd once shared thoroughly ranged,
the meal's convivial merriment over, the toasts,
emptied, they'd carry home disappointment they couldn't
define. *Enjoyable? Yes. But oh, how old so-and-so's changed.*

Learning

A learner, stalling at a traffic light,
queues backward cars. Greens yellow up to reds.
There, window-fixed in cameo-frame, a flight
of snowy-sprinkled steps holds newly-weds
arched by a porchway; he, in gaudy kilt,
she, fluttered white, lace held against a breeze
fresh-edged with April, holding head a-tilt.
The clicking cameras freeze a smile-now-please,
then off they go, confettied with the cheers
of relatives and friends – some smutched by harms
that lie across unchartered hopes and years –
life's longing for itself linking their arms.
May flesh so bond you nothing comes between,
I wish them, as the lights jump back to green.

Various Fulfilments

Pursuing happiness, psychologists say,
is what keeps people ticking. Some attain
it through religion, willing to defray
pleasure in this world for the fancied gain
of everlasting life in some beyond:
others, collecting match-boxes, or mats
for beer in pubs; or, on a public pond
sailing toy yachts; or breeding dogs or cats.
The rich race horses, while the betting poor
hazard their flutter on which wins or loses;
small boys find spotting trains has great allure,
while conjurors trick up illusioned ruses.
Honour to those who find contentment springs
from mastering the littleness of things!

The Course of Time

When I was six – and keenly I remember! –
each promised treat seemed aches of time away;
October yellowed into drear November
raw Winter, with its coldly wet delay
slowing down longed-for Christmas: Santa Claus,
mysterious as why I had to pray
each night beside my bed, though Santa's laws
proved wishes didn't always go astray.
With little left of distanced, caught-up time
for me to see and hear and half-belong,
I set my stamp of slowly-mastered rhyme
of what's now fast and weak, once slow and strong;
and savour each last cadence of delight
before the measured fall of timeless night.

For Rannoch, the Gentle Collie

You kept squirrel patrol, barking with rage
whenever the top of the grey dyke suddenly rippled,
or a bushy tail perked up, burying nuts
in the grass at the front of the house. You'd stand still,
the wind riffling your brown-white silky hair...

He even pees elegantly, the visiting
American Professor of Literature observed,
watching you pose on the hill to be photographed
for the anthology cover, *The Scottish Dog*...

At four o'clock every afternoon, your long nose,
capped with its widow's peak, nudged the reminder
that you, too, needed your daily dose of affection
before your dinner and stealthily carrying off
whatever the cats had left in their plastic dishes...

For fourteen years you companioned us, shedding your coat
on the carpet, clogging the Hoover's whirring spindle;
pacing through life, unconcerned, with your delicate feet ...

"A pity" I remarked in Paris or Salzburg,
"wherever Europa Nostra[1] meets you always
seem to have to leave us to go to funerals!"...
That's how it is, the Elder Statesman said.

[1]*Europa Nostra*, a confederation of voluntary conservation societies from
twenty-four European countries, whose Chairman from 1983 to 1989 was
Hans de Koster, formerly Defence Secretary, the Netherlands and Chairman
of Ministers, the Council of Europe.

An Elegy

A launch holds briskly out from the loch shore,
arrowing ripples. From a slowed-down turn,
a woman at the prow leans out to pour
ashes out of a silver funeral urn,
then, white and red, throws after, heads of roses
that float upon the patch of greyish rust;
hunched in the frozen posture grief imposes,
head bowed before the thinned dispersing dust.
Snorting, the boat churns up its normal pace
and chugs back where it started from, its wake
rocking the roses as a foam of lace
widens a trailing V astern, to take
roses and dust, so late the cause of weeping
into the water's wide anonymous keeping.

Fifty Years On
(for Joyce)

You are my heart's delight, the tenor sang,
hand-cranked on the holiday gramophone; for me,
gazing at your shy loveliness, words that rang
true, and in our garden by the sea
sterned my resolve to win your love and trust.
Children arrived to swell our married state
out of our eager lovings' innocent lust
that time could not unreference or abate.
Looking back now across experience
of pleasures, joys and sorrows, changes shared,
nearing life's final border customs fence
where hates dissolve and human love's unpaired
and privilege is forced to level ranks,
for such togetherness, my darling, thanks!

THREE FAIRY TALES FOR OUR TIMES

i

On listening to Gretry's 'Zémire et Azor'

Once upon a time an ugly beast
captured a father travelling with his daughter.
The father's urgent pleas to be released
met with the promise of impending slaughter,
unless the beast could make the girl his wife –
Playtex her girdle, *Maidenform* her bra,
Venus de Milo armed for modern life;
what stagey Frenchmen once called *oo-la-la*!
The father hurried home to break his word,
but she, being honest, hastened back unseen
to give the love she'd promised, when – absurd! –
a prince stood where the monstrous thing had been.
Girls, don't believe in fairy-tales. The prince
though shapely's, proved a monster ever since!

ii

In the Woods

A nubile little girl pulled on her hood
and cape of scarlet, as a good girl should,
to call on sick old granny, with a basket
of wholesome food. She, much too proud to ask it,
looked forward to such visits and the treat
the teen-age girl brought with her; things to eat,
having preserved a healthy appetite
though gnarled with arthritis, short of sight
and trumpet needed to assist her hearing.
The house she lived in, by a forest clearing –
her woodsman husband being long deceased –
nestled the end of a circuitous route,
through shouldered trees more quickly reached on foot.
Don't take the forest path, her mother warned her –
when giving good advice her daughter scorned her! –
You never know what might be lurking there;
some robber, tusky boar or grisly bear

(the story's set in some long distant time
when bears still roamed and people talked in rhyme).[1]

With basket on her arm, a youthful trot
out of her mother's watchfulness soon brought
the girl against the parting of the way.
The road through safety to the right-hand lay,
while to the left, the footpath's shadowed gloom
of leafy trees enticed her, saying "Coom":
(their seeds had blown upon an English breeze
from Yorkshire years ago). The promised ease
the mossy path afforded shapely knees
and delicate ankles, left her little choice.
Succumbing to temptation's leafy voice,
she left behind the safety of the road
and past dense tree-trunks delicately strode.

Soon after safe retreat was well behind,
the path seemed blurred and difficult to find,
the mouldered leaves of yester-year, a carpet
obliterating tracks. She thought: *How dark it
has suddenly turned!*, and longed to be with mother.
Next moment, hand on mouth, she tried to smother
(being polite) a rudely-uttered yell;
tripped by a hidden root, she almost fell.
Out from behind a bark both rough and thick
a creature sprang, as in a conjuror's trick;
long-toothed and hairy, half-a-wolf, half-man,
he held out paw-arms in a halting span.
Pretty maid, tell, he leeringly inquired
Where are you off to? All that she desired
was to get past his arms and run to granny.
But fear inspired an answer far from canny.
She told the truth and gave the full address
of granny's lonely dwelling; and in less
time than it took to add the postal code,
as if propelled by some invisible goad
the creature turned upon his laughing heels,
went racing off, but left a trail of squeals,
half-wolfish and half-human, thus suggesting
the route to follow where she had been questing.
At last she saw white walls through thinning trees,
a gentle chimney smoking lazy ease

42

and rushed to reach – surprise! – an open door.
She crossed the threshold and the rushy floor
to where her granny lay, her lacy mutchkin
hiding her features – as the case with such kin
is, just a wrinkled version of the girl's.
She, noticing her granny's old grey curls
were hanging lank, with justified surprise
said: *Granny, what remarkably big eyes
you've got.* "All the better to see you with,"
granny replied, in tones of manly pith.
Haven't your ears grown bigger? next was asked.
As ancients grow impatient being tasked
by children, granny's answer seemed too loud
as if she would appease a hostile crowd:
"All the better to hear you with." *Your hair
seems longer, too.* "It's rude to stare!"
And then your teeth... : Fed up with talk of dentures
when thinking of the stock of safe debentures
the long-dead father might have left his child
the wolf threw off the look he thought was mild,
and leapt from tossed-back sheets with an agility
that didn't go with granny-like fragility.
"All the better to eat you with," he shouted,
baring those things – and more! – that she had doubted.
Snarling his yellowed fangs – they needed brushing,
the girl thought – odd what funny things go rushing
fast-spooled, through minds of those who think they're dying
impression with impression swiftly vying!
"You needn't worry. I'm not going to beat you,
I'm merely going to strip you bare, then eat you."
With that he ripped her dress to work his will
before he fanged his evidential kill,
chewing her as a kind of sweet dessert,
tough granny, half-digested, still inert.
But as he stripped her naked budding torso,
she screamed and screamed and screamed, but always more so.
The woodsman who succeeded her dead father
was near enough to hear the frenzied lather
Red-Ridinghood created as she hollered.
Rushing inside the house, he quickly collared
the slavered wolf. Unleathering his axe,
upon its neck he gave three woodsman's thwacks,

43

turning the severed wolf-head's lusty growl
into a last despairing, dying howl.

The patient woodsman waited several years
until this girl-turned-woman's nightly fears
had been, by common sense and kindness, parried;
and then the two of them got safely married.

Though wolves don't speak in faultless human diction,
except in grim Germanic children's fiction,
and nowadays don't dress to go to bed,
eat grannies or small girls in hooded red,
they're still abroad in modern disguises
devouring innocence with fanged surprises.
So girls, don't mock your mother's good advice;
where eyes seem searching, mouths talk big, think twice:
not everything's a cuddle that looks furry,
nor shortcuts safest when you're in a hurry!

[1]Washington Irving, in his book *The Alhambra* (1832) writes:
'In these days, if anyone asked for bread, the reply was, make me a couplet: and the
poorest beggar, if he begged in rhyme, would often be rewarded with a piece of
gold... The people of Barbery, even those of the lower class, still make couplets, and
good ones too as in old times; but talent is no longer so readily rewarded.'

iii
The Rights of Property

I

In suburbs not a thousand miles from here
a widowed Mrs Smith lived with her son,
the clutch of poverty her constant fear
since, long ago, her husband had been done

to death; by whom, the police had never found,
stealing the wealth hard industry had earned.
Although they tracked through every inch of ground,
no trace of *why* or *where* was ever learned.

Poor Mrs Smith told Jack – the useless son
she'd scrimped and saved to spoil – at her wit's end
to feed them both with all their rations done,
that she would sell her cow and quickly send

him off to market with it, in the hope,
that he would bargain for a butcher's price.
So Jack set off, leading the cow by rope;
guileless, as yet not touched by human vice.

Halfway along the road he met a dealer
who dealt in profits (for himself, of course);
loud both in suit-check and deceit; a wheeler
whom years of phoney sales-talk had made hoarse.

Plunging his hand in his capacious pocket,
from out its depth he pulled a gaudy packet.
See, seeds of beans that shoot up like a rocket;
good protein, boy. With these you'll never lack it.

No one had told the boy things rarely grow like
the packet's wondrous perfect illustration.
Yours for the cow, the wheeler wheedled, shrew-like.
"Done!" Jack rushed home to show his sole relation

the bargain he had got her. All he kindled
was raging anger, boxing both his ears,
that out of shopping-money he'd been swindled.
Banishing Jack to bed, she dried her tears,

opened his bedroom window and threw out
the beans, then creaked upon her aged knees,
since superstition rendered her devout
to pray that silent God might grant some ease

to their predicament. By now, perspiring –
this Northern summer turned out oddly hot! –
she stripped herself of all her scant attiring,
let dreamful sleep impose its counter-plot.

II

Refreshed by sleep, Jack woke up in the morning
and pulled apart the curtains in his bedroom.
To his surprise, since he had had no warning,
a green translucent light filled out the said room;

not sunshine, raying its expected gold,
as flooded days not greyed by splashing rains:
what beetles in long grass might well behold
startled his gaze. He blinked and stared again.

A giant beanstalk with a clumpy root
rose up much higher than his neck could see –
the seeds his Mum threw out one thickened root,
its branches twined in step-like symmetry.

"Mother," he cried: "I'm off to climb the stalk."
You silly boy! You'll slip and tumble down
she argued, pleading. From such useless talk
she wiped her apron on a tearful frown.

Up, up he climbed, to reach that mythic sky
of fairy-tales and pious folks' belief:
which gives some credulous readers – Lord knows why! –
the promise of perpetual relief

from stress and strain and wrong down here below.
Up, up Jack climbed, to reach a desert plain,
a solitary castle lit to show
someone lived there. He knocked, then knocked again.

A mighty woman tugged the heavy door
inwards – he'd never seen a fleshly sight
so sizeable, and trembled to the core.
"I'll feed you, give you shelter for one night,"

she roared at him, then lugged him to her kitchen:
"for if my husband smells your human flesh,
he'll chew you up until you're grey as lichen."
Jack ate and drank her potage to refresh

his weary limbs; when suddenly, a roar
resounded. With a quite athletic shove in
that left him neatly doubled, cramped and sore,
he found himself inside her kitchen oven.

With soothing words the giant's wife dissembled –
Jack watched them through a ventilating grill –
with every munching chew the castle trembled,
the giant chomping his enormous fill.

Then, satisfied, he bade his wife go get him
his magic hen. When he commanded: *Lay*
the well-trained fowl, who didn't dare upset him,
clucked – and an egg of gold was on display.

Jack waited till the giant's heavy drinking
conduced, first drowsiness, then snore on snore.

46

He leapt out, grabbed the hen, and quick as winking
slid down the mythic stalk to reach earth's floor.

For many weeks the hen supplied the money
that lured them through their supermarket's aisles;
smoked salmon, pheasant, new-baked bread and honey
left them replete and happy. Until, whiles,

as often happens when there's sated need,
Jack once more climbed the bean-stalk, reconnoitring
what he might steal to gratify his greed.
This time, the giant's wife allowed no loitering

but in a panic, pushed him right inside
her linen cupboard. Through a wooden crack
Jack watched as nearer loomed the giant's stride,
a roar for food announcing he was back,

counting out gold and silver on the table
when gluttony again left him defenceless.
Biding his chance once more, quick Jack was able
to grab the gold and flee, this time not scentless.

Rich Jack became a business millionaire
take-over expert, rending jobs asunder;
for ruthlessness developing a flair;
an envied, sure financial nine-day's wonder.

And yet, despite the ease with which great wealth
came to him, he could not eschew fresh danger.
Risking his mother's happiness and health,
he climbed the stalk once more. The well-dressed stranger

the giant's wife set eyes on, had her puzzled.
This time, she crammed him in a copper kettle
the heavy lid of which should keep him muzzled.
This time, the giant showed more cunning mettle.

After his meal, this time he sang. Though sharp,
his somewhat tuneless wavering intonation
was matched by skill upon his magic harp.
Self-serenading leads, through susurration

to heavy sleep. Pushing aside the lid,
Jack grabbed the magic harp, which cried out "Master,
Master": then dropped it. Down the stalk he slid,
The giant chased him. Jack was much the faster.

"Mother," Jack yelled, pace gathering as he hurtled:
"go quickly. Grab for me a sharpened axe."
The widow had one by her, and much startled
watched Jack attack the beanstalk with hard thwacks.

Branches and leaves beneath the giant's bending
littered the lawn. His massive feet appearing
Jack was leant strength, thus with a last stroke sending
the roaring severed stalk to earth careering.

III

The moral of this fairy-tale's confusing,
for surely it is wrong to reap harsh gain,
the cost of which is other folk's abusing,
leaving a sense of loss and social pain?

But equally deplorable is stealing
with envy as the motive for our actions
when what we ought to strive for is the healing
of quarrelled faiths and disputatious factions.

Not even sclimming stalks till legs turn bandy
(though doubtless useful to the criminal classes).
or keeping sharpened axes always handy,
can fault where fiction over fact surpasses –
which is why stories fascinate the masses!

Friday the Thirteenth
(a canter in light verse for Mrs Kirsteen Stokes's pupils)

What lets twin-superstitions daunt you, pray?
Let's treat the question in an ordered way.

First, Friday. Romans in their sunny clime
called it the day of Venus, their sublime
Goddess of Love and Beauty. Further north,
bold Norsemen thought the day of equal worth,
the best day for a man to wed his bride.

Who caused the course of history decide
this lover's day should be undeified?
Why, early Christians who maintained that God
on Friday fashioned Adam from the sod.
Adam first ate the knowledge-fruit when Eve
allowed the devilled serpent to deceive.
On Friday, if Mohammed you believe;
then Friday was the day these first lives ended
as into storied legend they ascended.

So to the thirteenth. What peculiar lumber
of theoplasm makes a simple number
unlucky on a Friday, you may ask?
I'll answer, if I'm equal to the task.
Valhalla, where the Valkyrie once rode
and Nordic gods kept shadowy abode,
arranged a feast. Twelve gods were then invited;
but half-way through, their merriment was blighted
when Lokki, god of strife, gate-crashed the party.
Until that moment, all were hale and hearty;
but Lokki picked on Balder, god of light
and slew him in a most unseemly fight.
The downfall of Valhalla followed fast
which, cloud-constructed, wasn't built to last.

Another table in a different place
brought twelve disciples sitting face to face.
Their host, the thirteenth, come there to preside
was Christ, upon a Friday crucified
when Judas had betrayed and Peter lied.

All that was long ago, and can't affect
your safety. Be alert and circumspect;
don't kick black cats that cross you down the stairs
and break a leg; or pick a pin that flares
up at you from a rug and crick your back,
or trip upon a broken pavement's crack;
splinter your mirror with a hairbrush clout
if you don't like who's inside looking out;
forget your mascot, in a flustered fuss
step off the pavement underneath a bus;
or knock a painter's ladder by the feet

and end up horizontal in the street.

If these few simple precepts you obey,
you'll find, whatever superstitions say,
each thirteenth Friday's just another day.

Note
Theoplasm: the stuff from which god-legends are made.
See *Enc. Brit.* Article on "Superstition".

The Consumer's Hymn

People, they say, have stopped attending church,
so everywhere the congregation's shrinking,
God having left so many in the lurch,
famines and wars have set fresh doubters thinking,
and leave the ranks.

They go, instead, to some Aladdin's cave,
the nearest Supermarket of their choice
where *spend*'s the litany, not pursy *save*;
hushed muzak these cathedrals' soothing voice,
while weary shanks

trudge pharmacist, Post Office, even banks
to draw more cash; or nibble tasty snacks
when tired of roving corridors whose flanks
are lined with liberality's bright stacks.
Each trolley clanks

stiff wheels; each silvered mesh beneath the lights,
(soft as the puffed-out sound), till filled up, gleams
encouragement, while trade-description rites
proclaim that everything is as it seems
to please the cranks.

Sainsbury, Asda, Safeway, Somerfield,
fulfilling keen anticipation's goad,

long may your sweet temptations make us yield
however much our credit cards are owed,
we'll give you thanks.

The Sign

Once, in a pious holy place
where superstitions spun their role
of mummery and mystic grace,
and floating incense sponged the soul

of erring reason's disbelief,
a country girl knelt down alone
to pray her God would grant relief
from what, unmarried, had been sown

within her too-compliant womb
by any one of several men
(here, doubt at least had plenty room),
if she would never err again.

While breathing her unanswered pleas,
her senses leapt in sudden start;
though hearing neither cough nor sneeze,
some nearby statue loosed a fart.

Surprised, she gazed upon their features,
white, wishy-washy, meek and mild,
as are, they say, celestial creatures –
knights and their ladies, once reviled

for feudal cruelty when upright,
recumbent now, with folded hands
clasped in cold sleep; a peaceful sight
as if they'd claimed their promised lands;

virgins with child-in-arms; tough dames
renowned for rationing the need
of paupers begging pity's claims,
provided they obeyed her creed.

Just such a one – stout, amply-bustled –
although the marble never moved
from out her skirt's broad folds there hustled
an even louder fart: which proved

some thrifty goddess had been born.
The girl ran forth, ecstatic, shouting
that now a second Christmas morn
had just occurred. As she was "outing",

(to use the fashionable term
reserved for homosexual boasting)
the thought, of which she'd spread the germ,
burst into universal toasting.

Millions who felt their soul immortal,
would float, one day, in heaven's bliss,
swarmed through the nearest church's portal
to worship such a sign as this.

For several days each wormy-raftered
church with holy farting sounded;
its counterpoint, the merry laughtered
scepticism fate rebounded.

Against this oddly-backward notion,
used to pronounce what seemed divine,
much-baffled reason pled devotion
to gods, a discontinued line.

As sudden as this strangely shocking
noise had racked the dreaming spires,
it ceased, as did the foolish talking,
proving all superstitions liars.

What caused, some asked, this holy airing,
unless the simple girl pretended?
Why, too much fervent inner-staring.
Least said, they say, the soonest mended.

Note on *The Sign*
During September 1995, a girl follower of "the cruel Mahomet" (as David Hume
called him) claimed that on holding out a spoonful of milk to the statue of an animal

52

in a Mosque, the statue supped. The birth of a new holy man somewhere was inferred from this "miracle", and in mosques all over the world, hysterical men and women turned up with quantities of milk to explore the phenomenon. The explanation probably was that after the exceptionally dry summer the porous stone of the effigies absorbed a little of the milk, or, more probably, the milk simply trickled down the creatures' chests. After a few days of this manifestation, causing a shortage of milk for domestic use, the deity apparently became sated and the "miracle" evaporated. Years ago, when I was programme Controller of Border Television, the Managing Director, on the night we first went on air, insisted that an Epilogue be pronounced by the Anglican Bishop of Carlisle. Since the station served both sides of the Border, I insisted that there must also be a Scottish Epilogue, by the Reverend Dr George Macleod. "But you're an agnostic," the Managing Director protested. "Indeed", said I, "but I reserve the right to be a Presbyterian agnostic." Much the same goes for my attitude to supposed wondrous miracles.

Ah, Me!

Upon a time I read in some newspaper
a fine three-volume history of Scot. Lit.
had just been published. From a bookseller's shelf
I pulled it stealthily down, looked up the bit

about myself, and found that "modernism"
had passed me by; that I had just ignored
it. Dearie-me! But whitna thing to say
of one whom academic theories bored!

Had I not angered at distended bellies
bulging the dying bodies of the kids
that God so loved in Africa? Senseless murders?
Poetically speaking, lifted lids
off market-value pity? No blame taken?
Off piety's and politics' pretence?
Off tribal wars? Push-saturated sales
of arms (called, euphemistically, 'defence')?

Mocked at the things responsibility
discards like litter in the streets? Such platitudes
as bosses nosing troughed-up salaries?
The valueless glare of media attitudes?

Then, quite by chance, I read a learned journal
wherein a lettered one who taught the young
of literature's glories and delights,
revealed that "modernism" had been hung

upon its own petard, "post-modernism"
the theory that had now usurped its place.
Decently, she* proceeded to define it
to benefit the reading populace.

"A questioning of commonly accepted
values of our culture (closure teleol-
ogy and subjectivity),
a questioning that is totally dependent

upon that which it interrogates where the 'concept
of alienated otherness (based on binary
oppositions that conceal hierarchies)
gives way to that of differences, that is

to the assertion, not of centralised sameness,
but of decentralised community' and which
promotes a 'cultural democratizing
of high/low art distinctions and a new

didacticism', potentially radical
political questioning, contextualising
theories of the discursive complexity
of art, and a contesting of all

ahistorical and totalizing visions!"
Such a relief! What clarity she brings
to poets in the heat of celebrating
the shades of human joy, the tears of things!

* Linda Hutcheon: *A Poetics of Modernism* (1981), quoted by Christopher
Whyte in *Scottish Literary Journal*, Vol. 23 No.1.